Step Aside

A simple and effective guide for helping you get out of your own way

Kareem L. Williams

Step Aside

Copyright © 2017 Kareem L. Williams

Dedication

I dedicate this book to my loving mother, Roselind Williams. Through your strength and resiliency, I became the man that I am today. I am forever grateful and indebted to you. I love you beyond words.

To my hero—my big brother, Kerry Hall. You were, and will always remain my first example of what a responsible man looks like. I still strive to be as great as you.

To my lovely grandmother, Rose Mosely. You are such a blessing to our family. I wish I would've been a better grandson to you. By God's grace, I still have time left. I love you.

To my dearly departed uncle, James Bordley. There is not a day that goes by that I don't think of you. Can you believe it? Your "favorite nephew" wrote a book.

To my father, George Williams. I am so glad that we were able to strengthen our relationship over the years. I love you, pop.

And to all of my family and friends. Without you all, I would be nothing.

Kareem L. Williams

Special Thanks

Nicole Younger

Sheree Monroe

Marvin Kornegay

Latisha Bloise

Shannon Murphy

Khaliyl Corbett

Prentice Boone

LaToya Tyson

Brittany Yilmaz

Cynthia Brewster

Demetrice Armstrong

Dwight Burton

Gary Williams

Michiala Batson

Marcus Turner

Christie Speights

Andrew Haynes

Charles Grier

Kendra Jackson

Thank you all for supporting my dream!!

Table of Contents

Introduction

I would like to take the opportunity to thank you for investing in yourself by purchasing this book. By that action alone, I know that you want to live the best life possible. As I thought over the contents to put in this book, I asked myself how I could help others overcome the obstacle of self. Every word, sentence, paragraph, and chapter of this book has been carefully thought out based on my own personal experiences as well as research. I've spent countless hours reflecting on my life. The great times that we all remember so fondly, and the not so great times that we are sometimes embarrassed about. One thing that I've learned is that all of us have one thing or another that at times can hinder us from reaching the level of life quality that everyone deserves. On the flip side, I have learned that there is absolutely no excuse for us accepting mediocrity. We fully have the power to overcome any and every barrier that is set before us. In this book, I will provide several full proof principles that if properly implemented, will help you break free of life's struggles, including struggles that are self-inflicted. I want you to know that I value you. I value your time. I value your victories, as well as your shortcomings. I want to encourage you to be very open-minded while reading the text in this book. I am going to challenge you to be completely honest with yourself. As they say, the truth hurts. However, I believe that being truthful with yourself is a necessary "evil" when it comes to creating a life of abundance. So as you enjoy the pages of Step Aside, please know that above anything else I have your best interest in mind. I sincerely want you to get every possible lesson that is at your fingertips. Read it twice if you dare. If you can finish this book—and honestly say that you were not blessed by it—I will personally refund your money immediately. No questions asked. Please understand that this is not arrogance. Instead, it is the confidence of someone that has meticulously gone over every single aspect of the content within this writing, and believes 100% that it will help you be the successful person that you were put on Earth to be! So sit back, and enjoy as we work to help you get out of your own way!

CHAPTER 1

Am I guilty?

Welcome to Chapter 1 of *Step Aside* ! I think it is only right that I start off by explaining what it means to be in your own way. Simply put, I would define being in your own way as follows: If your decisions, behaviors, habits, relationship choices, etc. are holding you back from the successful life that you want, then I believe that it is you that is standing in your way. If this is the case, change is necessary in order for you to grow and be the awesome person you were born to be. When something is in your way, it is usually an inconvenience to you. For example, I absolutely hate sitting in traffic on the highway. It always seems to happen when I have somewhere important to be. In this situation, the cars on the highway are in the way of me reaching my destination.

Let us consider life's obstacles as cars in a traffic jam that we must get around in order to reach the life that we want—and more importantly—deserve. Sometimes an alternate route is necessary for us to navigate the heavy traffic ahead of us. We may be familiar with these other ways of getting to our destination, and other times we may have to use a GPS system to help us effectively arrive at our end point. Either way, if we want to get around these obstacles, some form of action must be taken.

It is very important for us all to at some point to be able to recognize if we are in fact holding ourselves back from a life of abundance. For instance, I struggled with drinking for years, and one day I accepted the fact that alcohol was coming between me and my dream. I didn't want to accept this, but it became a matter of asking myself, "What is more important to you?" Based on experience, it always seems hard to let go of the things that we enjoy most. Even if these things aren't good for us.

What is it that you could change that would immediately have a positive impact on your life? What vice? What bad habit? What decisions could you alter that would put you on that path to success that you yearn for? These are some of the questions that I had to ask myself. I encourage you to do some self-inventory in order to realize what changes must be made in your life. This is one of the hardest things to do. Taking a good look in the mirror will expose some of the ugly flaws that we all have at one point or another. However, the benefits of being honest with yourself will be a priceless investment that is sure to change your life.

So ask yourself, "am I guilty of being in my own way?" "Would I be better off if I let go of this bad habit?" "How can I change my ways, in order to get to a better place?" When you begin to face the truth of these questions, you have taken a step in the right direction. They say the truth hurts, and that honesty goes a long way. That couldn't be any truer than when you apply it to your own self-development. We have to accept our reality—good, bad, or indifferent—and take the necessary steps to change the trajectory of our path. On the next page

I ask that you do the following: Write down ways that you feel you are holding yourself back. For example, are you holding on to fruitless relationships? Are you a big procrastinator? Perhaps lazy? Whatever it is that you feel is in the way of your progress, write it down. This provides a good place to start the process of getting out of your own way.

**Write down ways that you may be in your own
way on the lines below:**

_____

_____

_____

_____

_____

_____

_____

_____

_____

Now that you have been honest with yourself about some of your shortcomings, I want to discuss some of the negative effects of us being in our own way. I believe that we all have been put on this Earth with a divine purpose to fulfill. Some people find their purpose early on. While others may find theirs later in life. What is of utter importance is that you do indeed find it. It is a matter of living an average life versus living a life of abundance.

When we get in our own way, we are ultimately throwing off what we were put here to do. Consider this sports analogy: When a quarterback sees a receiver that he wants to throw the football to, he releases the ball with the sole purpose of getting it to his target. That football has a purpose after leaving the quarterback's hand. The receiver has a purpose, and that is to catch the ball. In comes the defensive back, whose sole purpose is to stop that receiver from catching the football. His desire is to come between what that quarterback and receiver have purposed. At times we play defensive back in our own lives. Coming in between what is purposed for us and intercepting the success that awaits if we just stay on track.

For those that are not familiar with sports, I will give the following example: In school, we received many assignments and test from our teachers throughout the years. The purpose of these assignments was to provide us with knowledge that we would carry with us for a lifetime. But if you are anything like me, there were times that we didn't study, or give full effort when it came to schoolwork. Thus we came in between the purpose of the teacher as well as the assignment that was given to us.

The point that I am trying to get across here is that we must first find out if we are the cause of coming in between mediocrity and our ordained purpose. Secondly, we have to acknowledge the ill effects that it has on our lives. I don't know about you, but I want to leave a legacy. I want to tap into every ounce of potential that I possess. One of my favorite speakers, Les Brown, said that the most valuable place on Earth is a graveyard. It is full of people that went to their grave without ever realizing their true potential. By continuing to sabotage our own lives—and remaining in the way—we are adding to our chances of leaving this world without making the impact that we are capable of.

Imagine your life if only you were to make a few slight changes. A lot of times we aren't willing to start small. We try to take huge steps in the right direction, rather than taking small steps towards progress. I am guilty of this, and I know all too well the negatives of thinking this way. I would like to encourage you to try each day to take a small stride in the right direction. These small steps will become big steps. The next thing you know, you will, in fact, be completely out of your own way.

As this chapter comes to a close, let's do a quick overview. By now we understand what it means to be in our own way. Also, you have been honest about the ways that you are guilty of this. In addition to that, we discussed the negative effects that our ways may be hindering us from living the life that we deserve to have. Now that we have a better understanding, we can begin to work on methods and principles that are sure to remove us from being in our own way.

"At some point, I realized that it was, in fact, ME that was hindering my own success."

—Kareem L. Williams

Chapter 1 Notes:

_____

_____

_____

_____

_____

_____

_____

_____

_____

_____

_____

_____

_____

_____

_____

Chapter 1 Notes:

_____

_____

_____

_____

_____

_____

_____

_____

_____

_____

_____

_____

_____

CHAPTER 2

Taking Responsibility

I want to take a moment to discuss a dangerous game that I have played throughout various periods of my life. That game is called "The Blame Game." Are you familiar with it? On so many occasions, I looked to blame my misfortunes in life on others. For instance, I used to get into a lot of trouble at school. Just about every time that I got into trouble, I would blame someone else. If my teacher called my mother to say I was talkative in class that day, I would say that so-and-so kept talking to me. If I were suspended for fighting, I would be adamant in explaining that the other person started it. I absolutely would not take any responsibility for my troubles.

The bad part about not taking responsibility as a kid is that it followed me into adulthood. The cost of being irresponsible as an adult is much higher than when you were a child. As an adult, being irresponsible can lead to job loss, incarceration, financial struggles, and much more. For me, I didn't take heed to what I was taught about responsibility as a child. So when I got older, I continued to blame everything and everyone for my missteps. How often do you play the blame game? Be honest with yourself. When things go wrong, are you quick to own up to why it went wrong, or are you looking for the first person to point your finger at?

Blaming others for your wrong doings is a characteristic that we must remove from our lives. Winners take responsibility when things go wrong due to their own actions. I know that you consider yourself a winner. The simple fact that you are reading a self-development book says a lot. I want to encourage you to start taking a look in the mirror, and if things aren't going as well as you'd like due to your own actions (or inactions), you must place the blame on yourself and no one else.

Now let's talk about another reason we tend to put out there when it comes to us not living the life we desire. Circumstances. How often do you, or someone you know, say "I could have what I want if my situation were better"? I know I have said this many times in my life. For whatever reason, we become programmed to believe that our circumstances define us. Let me break the news to you: it is the other way around! We are in control of our circumstances. We must not allow them to control us. Do things beyond our control happen? Absolutely. Are we sometimes on the receiving end of unforeseen misfortune? No doubt we are. But what we have to realize is that these situations are only temporary. Circumstances change just like anything else. I implore you to learn how to adjust to life's circumstances and keep moving forward.

When I was 14 years old, I was arrested for armed robbery. I became a convicted felon before I was old enough to drive. At 17, I was arrested for what was initially attempted murder. In addition to that charge, I was also hit with firearm violations, assault, and about 7 other charges for this one incident. Before the age of 18, I had already accumulated a rap sheet that some adults never obtain. I was sent away from my family and loved ones for a total of about 2 years. These were some tough circumstances for a young man to be placed in, right? I could have easily let those circumstances define the rest of my life. I had a serious criminal record. I hadn't graduated high school. My life was absolutely ruined, most would think. However, I refused to let that be the end of my story.

By God's grace and mercy, I took my circumstances and used them to reshape and redefine my life. Today I don't have a criminal record. Not one single charge. I have a Bachelor's as well as a Master's degree. I am a business owner. I am an author. I have been blessed to be able to encourage people in multiple countries. I say all of that to say this: If I can overcome my circumstances, then so can you. I don't care what it is that you've been through. You have the power to overcome and change your life, but it starts with taking responsibility and then taking action.

This leads me right into my next point: NO MORE EXCUSES!!! That's right. NO MORE EXCUSES. I cannot stress that enough. There are way too many people in the world that have overcome seemingly impossible odds and found success afterward. I am one of them. Based on my own experiences—and the fact that I know there's nothing super special about me—I know you have the same ability to overcome circumstances. Even the ones that you create with your own decision making. So today is the day that I want you to remove all excuses from your mind. There is no such thing! You are great, and there is no reason why you cannot live a life filled with greatness. Now please do me a favor. I want you to put this book down for a second, and say the following out loud: NO MORE EXCUSES! I TAKE FULL RESPONSIBILITY OF MY CIRCUMSTANCES. I WILL NOT BLAME OTHERS. I WILL LOOK WITHIN. I WILL BE THE CHANGE THAT I WANT TO SEE IN MY LIFE!

"More people would learn from their own mistakes if they weren't so busy denying them."
—Harold J. Smith

Chapter 2 Notes:

_____

_____

_____

_____

_____

_____

_____

_____

_____

_____

_____

_____

_____

Chapter 2 Notes:

Mindset

The topic of mindset is one of my favorite discussions. For a long time, I didn't understand the importance of my mind. I didn't know how important my very own thoughts were. A huge part of why we stay in our own way for so long is the fact that we aren't willing to change the way that we think. In this chapter, I will discuss the effects of negative thinking, which in turn leads to negative living. Open up your heart and mind while reading Chapter 3 in an attempt to evaluate the way you have been thinking.

Mind over matter. You've heard that statement before, right? Well, let's dig a little deeper into what that means. Mind over matter means the use of willpower to overcome physical problems. For instance, working out can cause a lot of physical pain in your body. However, if you train your mind to focus on the results rather than the pain, in time, the pain will be bearable. We can apply this same thought process to emotional problems as well as physical. A lot of times when we are having trouble with something—or even someone—it is in our mind where the issue lies. If you already have it in your mind that you can't deal with something, you have already lost the battle.

For years I struggled with my own negative thoughts. Even today I sometimes slip into bad thoughts before I even realize it. What

I've learned is that once you replace these thoughts with thoughts of prosperity and good things, you are more likely to act on those things. Getting caught up in your own negative thoughts can be very costly. It is a very depressing state to be in. I know this from my own experience. A while back, I found myself in a real funk. I was miserable. I felt depressed and hopeless. I literally found myself sitting around, basking in a pool of bad thoughts. This lasted for about four months. During those four months, nothing productive came about. I wasn't working on my business. I wasn't making and/or cultivating quality relationships. I wasn't working on my gifts. I was simply hosting my very own pity party. My point in telling you that is this: nothing good ever comes out of allowing your negative thoughts consume you.

After months of non-productive living, I finally picked myself up off the couch and got back in the game. How, you ask? I simply realized that it was all in my head and that I was bigger than any lie my own mind could conjure up about me. You'd be surprised to find out how much of an enemy your own thoughts can be if not addressed. The moment I started to tell my mind to shut up, and that I was in control, is the moment that things started to come back together. So I need you to be encouraged when it comes to negative thinking. Hit the override button on your thoughts. Reset, and get back to a place where you think on things that are good. Things that involve the life of success and abundance that you know is attainable.

Another trait that can be a hindrance to your progress is complaining. We all have that one person in our lives that seems to do nothing but complain, complain, and complain some more. I will not pass any judgment though, because that person was once me. When life slaps us upside the head, the easiest thing to do is to complain. It takes minimal effort verbally, and absolutely ZERO effort physically. While we are complaining about our struggles, most likely we aren't taking any action to rid ourselves of them. Even if you are a great multi-tasker, doing these two things at the same time is near impossible. If we don't like the situation we are in, we must learn to complain less and do more! One thing that helped me get rid of my complaining ways was when I would hear someone else complaining constantly. I realized that this is what I sound like, and I needed to cut it out.

Complaining isn't a characteristic of a winner. A winner takes the punches and takes action not to get hit with the same punch again. A winner understands that struggles and disappointment are a part of life that we all must deal with. So instead of whining about why things are the way they are, a winner figures out how to change things. Part of getting out of your own way is to develop this mindset. Things happen. We cannot let these things control us to the point where we exude negative thoughts and actions. That only leads to further disappointment.

One other way—and in my opinion, the most important way—to shift your mindset is to speak victory, and not defeat. When you complain, you are giving fuel to the fire of failure. On the other hand, when you speak life over the situation, you are shifting things to work out in your favor. The Bible says that the power of life and death is in the tongue. This is so true. We must carefully watch what comes out of our mouths. When something isn't going the way we would like it to;

it is important that we speak on what we would like to happen versus what is happening. This goes back to the circumstances discussion from Chapter 2. Don't allow your circumstances cause you to speak death into your life.

"The mind is everything. What you think, you become."
—Buddha

"As a man thinketh in his heart, so is he" (Proverbs 23:7). Don't worry, ladies; this applies to men as well as women. This is one of my favorite verses in the Bible. It falls perfectly in line with having a positive mindset. If we think we are great, then we are. Even if our current circumstance doesn't exactly look or feel all that great. Greatness starts in the mind. It then gets ingrained in your heart, to the point that you actually believe in it. At that point, you will begin to speak greatness in your words. Naturally, what will come next is for your life to start taking on the characteristics of greatness.

Every day I speak words of encouragement over my life. This is called affirmation. Affirmation is defined as emotional support or encouragement. We all need this encouragement on a consistent basis in order to deal with the harsh realities of life. If we don't speak life into our situations, we can easily be blinded and distracted from our goals based on the world around us. Negativity is so rampant in the world that it is super important to think and speak positivity over your life. Here are a few examples of affirmations that I personally use. Feel free to apply them to your life, I assure you they will help. Say these things aloud daily:

1. I am amazing.

2. My day will be great today.

3. There is absolutely NOTHING that I cannot accomplish.

4. My future is bright.

5. I can overcome any obstacle in front of me

"I am unlimited in my wealth. All areas of my life are abundant and fulfilling."
—Louise Hay

Take a moment to write down a few of your own affirmations:

_____

_____

_____

_____

_____

_____

_____

_____

_____

_____

_____

_____

_____

_____

Chapter 3 Notes:

_____

_____

_____

_____

_____

_____

_____

_____

_____

_____

_____

_____

_____

_____

_____

Chapter 3 Notes:

Relationships

A huge part of the person you are now, and the person you will become in the future, depends on the relationships you keep. I'm not just talking about your girlfriend, boyfriend, or spouse. I mean every single person that you spend any significant amount of time around. At times we don't want to accept it, but the company we keep has a real impact on our choices. While we are our own individual selves, we still fall subject to outside influences. Especially from the people we are around the most. I cannot tell you how many times that I've made a decision based on the persuasion of a friend or relative. That is ok, as long as the decision is productive; but, as I'm sure we can all agree, sometimes bad decisions are made as well.

I would like to take a moment to discuss with you the three types of relationships. I give a big thanks to one of my mentors, Kendall Ficklin, for giving me his blessing to share these relationship principles with you. When he shared them with me, it hit me like a ton of bricks; and really put things into perspective about the relationships in my own life. It is my prayer that what I am about to share with you has the same type of impact that it had on me. It is a very simple breakdown on relationships, but powerful at the same time.

The first type of relationship is a parasitic relationship. According to Webster's dictionary, a parasite is described as an organism living in, with, or on another organism in parasitism. Parasitism is defined in Webster's dictionary as an intimate association between organisms of two or more kinds; especially: one in which a parasite obtains benefits from a host which it usually injures. I know that was a very scientific moment, but allow me to relate that to the company we keep. In the definitions relayed from Webster's dictionary, let's replace the organisms with ourselves and the people we know. If you are always benefiting from someone (or vice versa), and never contributing any value to their lives, you are equivalent to a parasite. When I say value, I don't necessarily mean monetary value. It could be emotional value. For example, providing some needed encouragement when the other person is struggling with something. It could be physical value, for instance, helping a friend move into a new house. To keep it simple, a parasitic relationship is one where one person takes, takes, and takes some more without ever giving anything. All the while draining the person that they are receiving from. These are the relationships to avoid!

The second type of relationship is a neutral relationship. In this relationship, neither party truly benefits from the other. The definition of neutral is a position of disengagement. A great example is a car. When that car is in neutral, it will not move forward nor backward. If the car is on a slanted foundation, you may get a bit of movement, but for the most part, the car remains stagnant. You can step on the gas as much as you'd like, but in neutral, the car will be still. The same exact thing applies to a neutral relationship. When two or more people are committed to a neutral relationship, nothing productive usually comes out of it. There is no forward or backward motion. Just idle. All involved parties tend to be satisfied with being average, or just getting by in life. Where is the benefit in that? You can do badly all by yourself!

"Associate yourself with people of good quality, for it is better to be alone than in bad company." —Booker T. Washington

The third type of relationship—and the type you should seek—is a mutual relationship. Mutual is defined as having the same feelings for one another. When this is the case, all involved parties understand their position and consider each other equals. They will not take advantage of each other. Their relationship will be give and take. These are the most powerful types of relationships. When the bond is a mutual one, things seem to get done. It is so amazing when two or more people with the same mindset and views—on how a relationship should be—come together. They create an unstoppable force. You know you can count on the other person(s) in all situations. If they can help you with something, they absolutely will.

Having heard the three types of relationships, what type is dominant in your life? Is someone draining you the way a parasite drains another organism? Better yet, are you doing the draining? Do you have relationships that you question what the purpose is? Have you been friends with someone for years, and nothing beneficial seems to come to either of you when together? These are some of the questions that you need to ask yourself. What you have to realize is that it isn't personal. Well, at least not in a bad way. You need to do inventory on who you are spending your time with, and make the necessary adjustments. You must do what is best for you. I have experienced many situations where the relationships I had with people just outgrew itself. That makes it easy. It comes naturally, and you just go your separate ways. However, sometimes you actually have to take action and let go of fruitless relationships in order to get to the next level. Later on in the book, I will talk about how you can also have relationships with things that are fruitless. Stay tuned.

One of my favorite sayings is that elevation requires separation. I get so excited when I hear that because it is so true. Sometimes, in order to grow, you must be willing to separate yourself from some people, places, and things. Imagine a hot air balloon. Before taking off, they are tied to the ground by thick ropes. The hot air balloon could never take flight without being separated from these ropes. Sometimes there are people in our lives that are that rope to our dreams. They tie us down with hopes that we will never elevate and reach our potential. On the other hand, there are also times when we are that rope to others. In either case, separation is required.

Another major benefit of creating and maintaining the right relationships is that you will have accountability partners. Mutual parties tend to uplift one another. Another one of my mentors, Nehemiah Davis, consistently checks in on me to make sure that I am doing the things that I say I am going to do. In return, I put the same pressure on him. We both know that we can count on each other for encouragement and accountability. It is always good to have people around you that will lift you up. I encourage you to create a circle of accountability if you don't already have one in place. In order to reach your full potential in all aspects of your life, you will need some help. Trust me; you can't do it alone. Having accountability partners played a role in me writing *Step Aside*. When I said that I was going to release my first book on my birthday (12-19-16), my immediate circle held me to that. Guess what? I did!

Do Not Be Deceived "Bad company ruins good morals." —1 Corinthians 15:33

To recap Chapter 4, keep in mind the following: There are three types of relationships—parasitic, neutral, and mutual. We need to weed out bad relationships that aren't producing anything beneficial to our goals and dreams. Mutual relationships should always be the goal. I encourage you to start things off with potential partners with the attitude that things are going to be mutual. Start by asking what you can do to bring value to their lives. This goes for business and personal relationships. Focus on being of service before you worry about what that person can do for you.

Understand that in order to elevate, you very well may need to separate yourself from certain people. Remember, it isn't personal. The choice to let go of anyone toxic and/or non-productive will only help you to grow. If it is you that is toxic to the other person, do them a favor and move on so that they can flourish. Don't be the reason for someone else settling for an average life because you surely wouldn't want that for yourself. Keep this analogy in mind: A lobster outgrows its shell several times in its lifespan. It becomes too big for the shell to contain, and the lobster must separate itself in order to continue growing. Be like the lobster, my friend!

Finally, never forget the importance of accountability partners. It is much easier to have a second (or tenth) push from others. You can never have too many people holding you accountable. Just make sure that these people are productive themselves. As the famous saying goes, "don't take constructive criticism from someone who's never constructed anything." The same goes for accountability partners. Listen to people that are responsible.

Chapter 4 Notes:

Chapter 4 Notes:

CHAPTER 5

Distractions

A distraction is a thing that prevents someone from giving full attention to something else. Achieving success will definitely require your full attention. It is not achieved when you constantly allow distractions to take you away from what you need to be focused on. When you think of the word distraction—and its definition—how many things come to mind for you? How often do you try to focus on getting something accomplished, only to be distracted? A few examples of distractions are TV, social media, people, phones, and at times circumstances.

We must develop the resilience and willpower to work on cutting down our distractions. This is no easy task, I assure you. But like anything else in this world, it is beyond possible. I myself struggled with blocking out distractions. There were times when writing this book that my phone would ring, or I'd receive a text message. I would abruptly stop writing, and answer my phone. After doing that, I would have trouble regaining my focus. So, to solve the problem, I started turning my phone off while writing.

One of the best ways to eliminate, or at least deal with distractions is to take action. In my example above, that action was to keep my phone off while writing. Another thing I did was unplug my television and placed it in my closet. I knew that if my TV was in sight, and ready for use, at some point I would turn it on. We must be intentional in our efforts when it comes to distractions. If you know that you are easily taken away from a task by something, the only way to handle it is to do something. If you don't, the distraction will continue to win.

With that being said, what are your distractions? Ask yourself this question, and then begin to figure out ways of eliminating, or at least controlling them. Things beyond your control will happen. This I understand. However, it is the things that we do have control over that seems to distract us the most. In other words, most times we make the choice to partake in things that take us away from our goals. For instance, I know I am not the only one who checks their social media accounts before stepping foot out of bed. Even though I know that the first thing I need to do is thank God for another day. It doesn't take long to be distracted, especially if the distractions are self-inflicted.

Here is one way that helps me to stay focused: I write down my daily task that I would like to get done. I list them in order from highest to lowest priority. I try to tackle the harder things first. Typically I would do this task first thing in the morning. The reason for this is because as the day goes along, you are more likely to be distracted. Let's say that you need to send out emails to potential clients of your business, and that is your most difficult task for that day. You need to formulate the email; gather all of your contacts; and finally send it. I would do that first thing upon waking up. Most people in your household are likely sleeping at 4 a.m., and if you live alone, then you are in even better position to get things done. After you've gotten the most difficult task done, you can now move on to what is next on your list according to priority level. Now as you move through the day, the tasks become easier, and the effects of distractions become less detrimental. For example, it won't really hurt you if you were about to take out the trash and you take a phone call. This distraction won't have long term effects.

"Starve your distractions. Feed your focus."
—Unknown

One of the most difficult things to do is to starve your distractions. I find it that I typically enjoy most—if not all—of the things that distract me. I am not tempted to stop working on an important task in order to go listen to a lecture on the molecular structure of soil. That is because I have absolutely ZERO interest in that subject. However, if one of my good friends invites me out for cigars, I would find it hard to say no. That is because I like to have a nice cigar and converse with good company. So it is of little importance to be able to say no to things that don't peak your interest. It is when you like—and sometimes love—the distraction that your will power must kick in.

I believe that your focus has to stay fixed on the end results. When you can see the end of what your task will mean to you, you are more likely to remain focused. Writing *Step Aside* was one of my biggest goals. It was also the most difficult thing that I've ever done. However, I knew that this book would change my life, as well as the lives of others. Knowing this made it all that much easier to block out anything that took me away from the task of writing. You have to want that end result so bad that nothing, and no one, will stand in the way of getting it done. A good way to do that is to write down the task, what it will take to get it done, and finally what the end result will mean for you and those around you. This will give you a complete view of the task, and make it much easier to stay focused. Distractions have come between many great ideas and caused those that had the ideas to be unsuccessful in bringing those ideas to fruition.

Are your dreams bigger than your distractions? Of course they are. Dreams of changing the world. Dreams of changing the lives of millions of people. Dreams of making the lives of your family better. These are all great dreams to have, and they are all most definitely bigger than any distraction that may present itself. Developing the courage and the fortitude to push through them is what will separate you from being average and being great. The greats are successful because they knew how to starve their distractions and feed their focus. Do you think Kobe Bryant allowed someone's tweet about him to distract him from putting up a thousand jumpers in the gym daily? Or did Floyd Mayweather allow watching his favorite TV show to keep him out of the gym? I highly doubt it. This is why these types of people become and remain great at what they do.

You have that same greatness inside of you. The moment you realize that, you will begin to live life in a different way. You will understand that what you have set out to accomplish — far outweighs any type of distraction you face. TV will become irrelevant. The latest trending topic on social media won't grab your attention. What someone else is doing will not be of any concern to you. That is because you have figured out how to starve your distractions. I encourage you right now to stick to the plan that you have for your life. Walk in your purpose, and let nothing come between you and the end result that you seek! Your future self will surely thank you. Write down all of the things that distracted you from completing important goals, and then write down how you will eliminate them going forward.

Chapter 5 Notes:

Chapter 5 Notes:

_____

_____

_____

_____

_____

_____

_____

_____

_____

_____

_____

_____

_____

_____

Developing Better Habits

There is one other huge thing that separates average people from the greats. That thing is the habits that a person has on a day-to-day basis. Someone that gets up at 4 o'clock in the morning tends to get more work done than the person that rolls out of bed at noon. A person that reads often is more likely to have more knowledge and wisdom than the person who never reads. Developing the habits of a winner will put you in a better position to achieve the great success that you seek.

The first step to better habits is acknowledging the bad habits that you currently have. For me, one of my bad habits was smoking. I picked this up when I was fourteen years old. This bad habit attached itself to me for the next twenty plus years. I know the effects of it, and how detrimental it is to my future. Yet I still allowed myself to partake in it. What bad habits are you struggling with? Habits that you know will benefit you in a major way if you were to let them go. Do you have a habit of being lazy? Perhaps you have a habit of being close-minded. Maybe your bad habit is dealing with the wrong types of people. Whatever your bad habit may be, I suggest that you figure it out, embrace it, and work on replacing it with a habit that is conducive to where you are headed.

It is of great importance that we understand our bad habits, and realize in what ways they are affecting our lives. I am a fast food junkie. I absolutely love the greasy indulgence of a cheeseburger and fries. Or a hot order of chicken wings from the local Chinese store. However, I am in tune with how this habit of eating out affects my life. One way is my health. I know that eating this fattening food isn't the best for my body. Another negative impact takes place in my wallet. It is super expensive to eat out every day. Just imagine if we spend twenty dollars a day on food on the go. Let's do the math. $20 X 30 days = $600/month. Now imagine if I would go grocery shopping instead, and spend about $150 monthly. That would open up $450 that I could invest elsewhere.

Evaluating your habits—and their effects—will help you become a better person in business, relationships, and life in general. Some say that it takes twenty-one days to break a habit, and/or create a new one. That number varies depending on who you ask. One thing I do know is that when you do something consistently, it eventually becomes a habit. Are you willing to break your bad habits and adopt new ones in order to grow? This issue is similar to what we talked about in Chapter 4. We have to realize that our dreams and goals are far more important than any bad habit that we have developed over the years.

Accepting your bad habits will take honesty. We must be open and honest with ourselves in order to move on to better habits. Like I said before, the truth hurts. Lying to yourself hurts much more. I struggle with using profanity for instance. I work on cleaning that up on a daily basis. The fact that I realize I have this bad habit allows me to work on fixing it. We simply cannot fix something that we aren't willing to acknowledge is broken. That is self-development 101. So take a moment to ask yourself: "What habits do I need to rid myself of to take my life to the next level?"

"All bad habits start slowly and gradually, and before you know you have the habit, the habit has you."
—Zig Ziglar

Bad habits become second nature if left unattended. The quote on the previous page holds much truth. A lot of times we don't even realize that we have adopted a bad habit. We become so used to doing something that it becomes almost second nature to do these things. We don't need an invitation or a cue. We simply do them. No one needed to tell me that it was time for a cigarette after a meal. I was so used to smoking after eating that I naturally reached for my pack after I took the last bite. In other words, the habit had me!

If we are going to allow our habits to have us, let's work to be sure that they are good habits. Habits that will lead us down a road of success, and not down a path to disaster. Laziness is a path to nothing. Procrastination takes you nowhere. Treating people wrong only brings about strife and pain. We must let go of habits such as these if we ever want to reach our full potential. Everyone who has ever failed at something surely has had bad habits to at least place some of the blame on. Am I saying that if you develop good habits, nothing will ever go wrong in your life? Or that you will succeed at every single thing that you do? Absolutely not. What I am saying is that good habits raise your chances of leading a better quality life if implemented and maintained.

Now that we have discussed bad habits—and how they play a role in our lives—let's now move on to talk about ways that we can adopt better habits. The key is that we cannot despise small beginnings when it comes to making changes for the better. Sometimes we expect change to come overnight, when the reality is that a small step taken daily is what will lead us to our destination.

One of my favorite quotes is: "Even a thousand-mile journey begins with one step." This quote is very inspirational for those of us that tend to try and build Rome in a day. I myself have a history of trying to stop bad habits cold turkey. I tell myself when I wake up in the morning that I am never partaking in that bad habit again—when the reality is that if I slowly work to get rid of the habit, the likelihood of me sticking to it increases. I want to advise you to work on taking small steps when it comes to making necessary changes in your life.

One of my biggest misconceptions about breaking bad habits was thinking I could break them overnight. I would say I'm quitting gambling tomorrow, for example. The likelihood of doing something so sudden was very low. Bad habits take time to form. They also will take you some time, and extra effort, to get rid of them. The upside to this fact is that the same thing applies to good habits. The more you do them, the more they become a part of you. So stop beating yourself up when that bad habit seems to be impossible to overcome. With time and small steps forward, you will eventually rid yourself completely of that thing that's been holding you back.

Here is an exercise that I want you to try: Pick one of your bad habits. Effective immediately, I want you to start working towards ridding yourself of this habit. If it is procrastinating, I want you to carve out ten minutes a day to work on a task that you've been putting off. I know ten minutes doesn't sound like much, but ten minutes is ten times more than what you've been doing. If you haven't been reading at all or as much as you'd like, I want you to commit to reading two pages daily. Two pages is a small task, but the point is to develop a better habit slowly and consistently until it becomes second nature. After you do this, you will be able to up the ante and take on more. Maybe after a week or so, you can start dedicating thirty minutes a day to working on that task. Instead of reading two pages a day, you can now move up to five pages a day. Before you know it, you will have developed a good habit that is sure to help you grow into the person that you are trying to become.

Habits separate the good from the great. Whatever it is that you want to do with your life will heavily depend on the habits you adopt. So make developing the habits of a winner one of your main priorities.

We must realize that to progress in life, we will have to consistently display positive behavior. Bad habits will get you nowhere. I have learned that the hard way. Work slowly towards swapping out the bad habits that hinder you for good habits that will help you grow.

Chapter 6 Notes:

Chapter 6 Notes:

CHAPTER 7

The Four B's

A great tool to assist you in getting out of your own way is to develop principles. When you have standards and principles in place, you are better equipped to grow into the person that you are meant to be. In this chapter, I will discuss four principles that have helped me in a major way. I encourage you to adopt these principles in some form or fashion. However, don't hesitate to create your own personal list. I am in no way trying to tell you what to do. I am simply telling you what worked for me.

The four B's of success are belief, begin, benefit, and blessing. Through experience, I have realized that these four things really have helped me become who I am today. I will take some time here to go over each principle. I will explain what they mean to me, and how using them has helped me tremendously. I do understand that the readers of this book will come from different backgrounds, ethnicities, professions, etc. In addition to that, we all have different perspectives on what success is. Success for some may be building a profitable business. For others, it may be overcoming a vice that has hindered you. My point is that this book doesn't just apply to success as far as business goes. It is related to success as you see it. So let's get into the four B's.

The first B is belief. I think that the first step to being able to accomplish anything is to have the belief that you can do it. I mentioned in this book that I have always had people in my life that believed in me. That didn't matter one bit until I started believing in myself. So you must realize that your faith in God, and in yourself is a huge factor in where you want to go in life. If you do not believe that you can do something, there is nothing in the world that will give you the ability to do what it is that you set out to do. You absolutely have to have the faith necessary to tackle the task. It doesn't have to be a large amount of faith. The Bible mentions of having faith the size of a mustard seed. To be more specific, in Matthew 17:20, the Bible says, "if you have faith as small as a mustard seed, you can say to this mountain, 'Move from here to there,' and it will move. Nothing will be impossible for you."

That scripture is so profound to me. It helps me understand that sometimes we must go scared. What do I mean by go scared, you ask? Here is an example based on my personal experiences: I am a public speaker. Most times that I go speak to a group, I am nervous. My heart is racing. My palms are sweaty. At times I am even shaking. Regardless of all of these things, I have faith in God and in myself to know that I am more than capable of delivering a great speech to my audience. Don't think that belief in yourself will mean that you are fearless. It doesn't mean that you will prevail in every situation. What belief does is, it gives you the chance to go after opportunities that others won't.

Some people are so scared of failing that they pass on opportunity after opportunity. They don't believe in themselves enough to venture out of their comfort zone. The great Hall of Fame hockey player Wayne

Gretzky once said, "You miss 100% of the shots you don't take." You have to have just enough faith in yourself to at least take the shot at what you want. So how confident are you in yourself? What limits have you been putting on your abilities based on a lack of faith? How many opportunities have passed you by simply because you didn't believe you were capable of handling it? Today I want you to abandon the mindset of doubt. I want you to start taking shots, even if your faith is only the size of a mustard seed! I can almost guarantee that you will see an immediate difference in your life. Opportunities that you once overlooked will seem like a small task to you. Your confidence will rise. Challenges will become chances to show your greatness!

The next B is to begin. After developing confidence and faith in yourself, the next thing you must do is begin to take action. As I said previously, you cannot do anything without first believing that you can. Now that you believe, it is time to put that belief to work. Without action, your belief holds little value. The moment I started to believe that I could actually own a business, I started putting in the work to make it happen. I stopped procrastinating and making excuses for why it wouldn't work. I realized that I had the power and the ability to do any and everything that I put my mind to.

Every single thing in this world started with a beginning. Having ideas are useless if you never begin to bring that idea to fruition. I've met countless people that have great ideas, but they haven't even put them on paper. The idea is stuck in their head. Keeping an idea in your head is like a woman being pregnant for her entire adult life. A seed was planted in her. This seed is a beautiful being that absolutely needs

51

to come into this world. If the labor process never begins, the seed will never be able to make an impact.

Think of your ideas and goals as beautiful lives that have been planted inside your head. Realize that these ideas and goals will not be of any benefit unless you begin to birth them. Stop wanting things to happen, and start making them happen. Do not despise small beginnings. Don't feel bad if what you want has only been written down on paper. That is a start. The Bible also says to write down the vision and make it plain. When your vision for something is in plain view, you have a better chance of taking the necessary action to make it a reality.

It is a shame when we put our dreams and visions to the side all because we aren't willing to start. When I decided that I was going to write a book, it seemed like a daunting task. I thought about the hours of writing it would take. I saw the process as difficult. It was something that I had never done before. Once I accepted that this is what I wanted to do, I started taking the proper actions to make it happen. You are literally reading the results of me taking action on a goal of mine. Had I not first believed, and then took action, this would not be possible.

So I encourage you to get started today! Whatever it is that you envision for yourself begins now at this very moment. Don't waste another second procrastinating. Your destiny awaits you. Waiting to start is a disservice to yourself as well as those that depend on you. Understand that your purpose involves more people than yourself. Don't be selfish by sitting on that great idea you've had for years.

Don't deny yourself anymore opportunities because you thought you were unfit to take them on. Believe in yourself, and begin to show it by taking action! Do it today!

"Action is the foundational key to all success."
—Pablo Picasso

The third B is the benefit. Now that you have tackled doubt and procrastination, you should start to see the benefits of your lifestyle changes. Deciding to change your ways isn't in vein. I wouldn't be sharing these principles with you if I didn't feel that they would benefit you in any way. These principles are sure ways that have helped me to get out of my own way. I was so full of doubt and laziness that I was holding myself back from benefits and opportunities.

One of the benefits of the first two B's is the confidence you gain in yourself. It is a great feeling to believe that you are capable of achieving even the biggest of dreams. It isn't a feeling of arrogance. Arrogance is a negative attitude. However, confidence is a great characteristic to adopt. When you believe in yourself, you walk differently. You talk differently. Everything about the way you carry yourself begins to change. That is a huge benefit, and it gives you a significant advantage over the average person. Like I said, there are so many people in the world who don't have faith in themselves. Your confidence will begin to set you apart from the rest. That is a benefit worth having.

Another benefit of taking on these principles is that fact that you will attract quality people into your presence. Greatness recognizes greatness. Not many people want to be around those that lack confidence in themselves. No one wants to hang out with a slacker. Just about everyone who has dreams and aspirations wants to hang out with confident, action oriented people. When I was lazy and I doubted myself, I just wanted to be alone. I would literally dwell in my apartment for months at a time. It would be just me and my thoughts. I didn't want to be around anyone, and I surely didn't want to be around anyone that was the opposite of me at that point. I felt like I wasn't worthy of hanging around confident go-getters because I wasn't one of them.

When I changed my mindset and developed the ability to believe in myself, the type of people I needed around me started to fall into my life. The benefit of having great people in your life is that you can bring value to each other. Relationships are everything. You want to attract like-minded individuals into your presence. You do that by being a confident, action oriented individual. The more I implemented these four principles into my life, the more I started to see the benefits of doing so.

The last benefit that I will discuss is the financial benefit. This is very relative if you are a business owner. It also is helpful if you are in a sales driven career or industry. My sales in my business went up once I became confident in my brand. There were times when I would be at an event, and because I lacked confidence, I wouldn't engage people to network. When I should've been working on building customer relationships, I was either on my phone or talking to someone I was already familiar with. This would result in plenty of missed opportunities to sell my product. When my confidence changed, so did my sales. I gained the ability to be bold and approach potential clients. I realized that the worst answer they could give was a no. As a result, I sold more products. Belief and beginning to reach out more ultimately led to some financial gain. There are plenty of other benefits that you will reap from implementing the four B's. These were just a few of mine.

The final B is the blessing. No, I am not talking about the blessings that you will receive by practicing these principles. I am talking about the blessing you will now be for others. I need you to understand that the name of the game is service. Every gift, talent, and ability that you have been given is meant to bless, and be of service to others. When I finally realized this fact, my whole perspective on life changed. I stopped worrying so much about finances. I didn't care if I was noticed. I had no interest in much other than how I could be of service. When you serve others, all of the things that you desire will come to fruition.

I say that to say this: These four B's are a great tool to use. However, I believe that these principles are a prerequisite to allowing you to bless other people. If you have no faith in yourself, how can you help anyone else? If you are a slacker, and never take action, how can anyone benefit from that? If you aren't receiving any benefits in your life, how can you be beneficial to anyone else that needs you? You cannot pour from an empty cup. But when you are full of confidence, action, and fruit (benefits), you are more than capable of blessing those around you.

I truly hope that you have taken these words in and that you will begin immediately to at least try using what you've read. Again, I can only tell you what I know based on what I have experienced. Even so, I am beyond confident that what worked for me will work for you as well. I don't refer to this book as a simple guide for no reason. It is my aim to provide you with practical, simple ways to add value to your quality of life. So embrace these four B's, and if and when they work for you, please pass them on to others that need them.

Chapter 7 Notes:

Chapter 7 Notes:

CHAPTER 8

Consistency

It is my hope that by now you have learned several ways to help you get out of your own way. Now I want to talk to you about a major word that will help you remain out of the way of your own success. That word is consistency. Consistency is something that I've struggled with over the years. I would have a six-month run of greatness, followed by two to three months of average to poor activity. Being inconsistent can happen for many reasons. A major life event such as childbirth may happen. Something like this can and will change the way you live your life. However, having success does not allow much room for time off.

Allow me to share a story about how inconsistent behavior affected my small business. When I first started Positive Vibes Only—my first business—it took off. I was getting a lot of support, and my following was showing steady growth. This went on for about three or four months. After that time had passed, I fell into an unwanted state of depression. Nothing dramatic happened in my life to cause this. Depression is something that I've dealt with in my adult years. In this instance, it caused me to totally neglect my business. I wasn't engaging my customers. I wasn't seeking speaking engagements. I basically went off of the grid for a few months.

After seeking help for my depression, I came back on the scene expecting everything to pick up where it left off. Do you think it went as planned? Absolutely not. It was like I had to start over from square one. I didn't quite understand why starting over was necessary being as though my first few months went so well. I soon realized the importance of consistency. Consistency is especially important when you have a business where people depend on you for encouragement and uplift. That experience taught me several things. One of those things was that in order to stay consistent, you need to be proactive.

If you know there are things that you struggle with, such as depression, laziness, fear, medical issues, etc., you have to know your triggers. Now when I feel like I may be slipping into a phase of depression, I take the proper steps to ensure that there are no hiccups in my personal life or business activities. I now realize the importance of staying consistent. Consistency is one of main the things that people take a strong look at when dealing with a person. It really is a major factor in business, relationships, and life in general.

I will use a sports figure as an example. If LeBron James suddenly averaged eight points per game for a few games, we would wonder what was wrong with him. We would say things like, "He's losing it," or "He's getting old." We have become so accustomed to him scoring twenty plus points per game on a consistent basis that anything less wouldn't be normal. Great people are expected to do great things on a consistent basis. If you are—or want to become great—you must realize that you will be expected to show up consistently. Those that look to you as a leader will expect nothing less from you. This is one of the reasons that people say they want to be great, but never make it a reality. They have a hard time showing up, and displaying the characteristics of someone great on a consistent basis.

Results are another major reward of being consistent. Once you start to see the fruits of your hard labor, it becomes almost addictive to be consistent in your ways. For example, when you see your body transforming from your consistency in the gym, isn't that a great feeling that your efforts are producing results? That same process goes for every area of your life. When you consistently work at something, it is bound to pay off. You reap what you sow. Please be mindful that you also can reap bad things. If you consistently sow bad seed, you will reap a bad harvest.

I need you to pride yourself in your ability to be consistent. Your success will be measured a lot by your ability to keep pushing. There will be many obstacles in your path. But one of the greatest weapons to overcome obstacles is consistency. Consistency builds momentum. So when a barrier presents itself, you have enough momentum to run straight through it with minimal damage. For instance, you have been saving money for a rainy day for the last six months. Your rainy day arrives, and your car catches a flat tire. This is a minor thing to you because you know that you can easily replace the tire by tapping into your rainy day savings. If you hadn't been consistent with your saving, this flat tire would've been much more of a burden. I used that example because there was a time that I had to call my loved ones if any emergency presented itself. It wasn't a good feeling at all, and it encouraged me to be more responsible with my finances.

61

The best teacher in life is experience. A lot of times we have to experience the damage of inconsistency to realize the errors of our ways. Nothing good comes from being inconsistent. When you are hot, then cold, and then hot again, that causes your life to be like a roller coaster. This roller coaster isn't a ride that you want to get on. It is a roller coaster of failure. You aren't a failure, so I urge you to find that steady momentum in your life. It is the only way that you will grow into the person that God intended for you to be.

Your determination to succeed will also drive you to stay consistent. When you truly understand that you are in control of your destiny, you will find the fortitude to stay on track. I am literally driven by my God-given purpose. Knowing that God has great plans for me pushes me to be as consistent as possible. The Bible says that faith without works is dead. I need my faith to be consistent; therefore, I need my actions to match my faith. I urge you to do the same. Be totally in tune with the fact that these two things go hand in hand. Once your actions are consistent, your faith will align with that. This will lead to better days than you've become accustomed to seeing.

I truly want readers of this book to embrace the fact that greatness lies within you. It is patiently waiting for you to notice it. Your greatness will not suddenly come out of you unprovoked. It also will not show up if you aren't sure of yourself. You show that you believe in your greatness by consistently displaying great behavior. Once God sees that you are serious about wanting to be great, He will allow what's been inside you all along to show to the world. The world we live in is in desperate need of people like you. People who have been holding back their abilities. So many people have not been recognizing their true potential. So many people have been in their own way for way too long. The time is now for you to reveal yourself, and be who you are meant to be!

"We are what we repeatedly do. Excellence, then, is not an act, but a habit."
—Aristotle

The quote by Aristotle on the previous page is, in fact, one of my favorite quotes of all time. So many times we think that we can simply become great at something without putting in the necessary work to do so. We believe that if we work hard for a few months—or even years—we will be at our best, and have a life of abundance. Does this work for some people? Absolutely. However, more often than not, greatness takes years and years of consistent actions. Michael Jordan didn't become the greatest basketball player of all time (in my opinion) by practicing for a few months. He worked on his craft and cultivated his God-given talents for years to become the player he was. He understood the importance of consistency.

You can be the Michael Jordan of your field. That may be at your job, or perhaps as an entrepreneur. Whatever path you decide to take, just know that you will need to adopt consistency as one of your main principles. The foundation of what you choose to do needs to include this to thrive. Your foundation of principles will take you far in anything that you do. Be sure to develop a list of core values that are dear to you. Learn not to compromise them for anything. Your principles will develop your character. Your character will mean everything. A few of my values include integrity, service to others, compassion, and of course CONSISTENCY!

Chapter 8 Notes:

_____

_____

_____

_____

_____

_____

_____

_____

_____

_____

_____

_____

_____

_____

Chapter 8 Notes:

Your Purpose Is a Priority

It wasn't until I finally stepped aside that I began to find God's purpose for creating me. When you are constantly in your own way, you are blocking the second most important day of your life.

It is said that the two most important days in your life are the day you were born, and the day that you figure out why you were born. Once you figure out your purpose, you become an unstoppable force.

Purpose is defined as the reason for which something is done or created, or for which something exists. For instance, cars were created and built as a means of transportation. They were designed to allow us to travel from one point to another in an efficient manner. Transportation was and is a car's purpose. Just like a car, God designed and built us with a specific purpose in mind. We are not here simply by chance. That is my whole-hearted belief.

One of the worst things that a man (or woman) can do is to never figure out what their purpose is. In purpose lies the ability to change the world. Without having one, life is just like a story without that great ending. There are so many people that go through life never realizing what lies inside of them. They simply go through life fitting in with the norm. They never stretch themselves or step out of their comfort zone.

This is not the life you were created to live.

Not finding your purpose does not mean that your life will be bad. Or that you yourself are a bad person. What it means is that you will never fully experience the great life God created you to live. God wants us all to live a life of abundance. We were not put here to simply "get by." For years I lived my life with no purpose. I went about my days with no true sense of where I was going. I wasn't really concerned with who I was, or why I was put here. Life for me was lived on a day-to-day basis, and I was content with simply existing. I want to relay a very important message to you right now: YOU WERE NOT BORN TO JUST EXIST!! Your creation has so much more meaning than that.

I believe that most people hit a point in life where they ask the question, "Why am I here?" It is probably one of the most asked questions in the history of man. It is a very good thing to want to know. If you are wondering what you are here for, then that is a great step in the right direction. Many people never even care to ask this question. What they don't know is that finding out the answer will unlock so many great things about them, and what the future holds for their life.

I didn't start asking myself what my purpose was until I was in my thirties. Up until that point, I can honestly say that I didn't care much. Again, I was content with merely existing. I was ok with going through this life without making any true impact in the world, or in the lives of others. It wasn't until I became frustrated with going in circles that I began asking God the question, "Why am I here?" I found myself making the same bad decisions year after year. I found my mood, and behavior, on a constant roller coaster. I realized that if this way of life continued for me, I would surely become a failure. Just a few years ago, I was at rock bottom. I was entangled in a web of addiction, depression, confusion, and misery. The worst part about that is that I was in complete denial. I didn't really see these things as the debilitating problems that they truly were.

I knew that I needed to do better, but I was deceiving myself by believing that these issues were not a big deal. I constantly justified my behaviors and told myself that the problems would solve themselves. This is not the way that life works. If we never make a conscious effort to make changes in our life, it will never happen. Understand that external change first requires internal change.

Realizing that I was on a path of self-destruction, I started to completely doubt myself. I wondered if I would ever change my ways. In fact, I wondered if I even had the ability to do so. It got so bad that I wanted to end my life. I was so frustrated with the self-inflicted pain that I was going through. I felt like there was no need for me to continue living. I thought to myself, *why should I keep going if all that I seem to do is ruin things?* My finances were in total shambles. I lost my apartment due to my gambling addiction. I was deeply depressed. I tried daily to erase my pain by smoking and drinking. I will be the first to tell you: your problems are there waiting for you after you sober up.

One day I woke up and realized that something needed to change and that it needed to change quickly. I had no idea what to do, or how to do it. All I knew was that my life needed some drastic changes if my life was to get better. I began to get around people that seemed to be living a life that I wanted. I stopped isolating myself. I realized that the more time I spent alone, the more miserable I became. These may seem like small changes, but they were actually the first steps towards me finding that breakthrough I so desperately needed.

One day a friend of mine made a suggestion. He thought that I should start posting inspirational videos to my social media accounts. I had always been very transparent about my struggles with life, and he believed that there were people out there in the world who needed to hear my story. I was initially hesitant to do this. "Why would anyone want to hear about my issues?" I asked myself. I figured that people already had enough problems of their own. Why should I add to that?

For years, people around me had been telling me that I had a powerful story and an even more powerful voice. The thing is, I didn't believe them. I could not see myself actually being a positive influence to anyone. Everything about my life was negative. At least that's what I thought. Even though I felt like I shouldn't, I decided to take my friend's advice. I started sharing my testimony on my social media. I was very open and honest about my struggles with alcohol, drugs, gambling, and other vices that I felt were holding me back. To my surprise, I received great reactions from the people who followed my accounts. This brought me great joy to know that my story was helpful and valuable to others. The best part is this: I had found my purpose.

All of the years that I was ignoring my gifts, I was, in fact, running from my God-Given purpose. Now some may consider that as time wasted. However, I believe that I just wasn't ready to accept my purpose. I believe that people find out what it is that they were put on Earth to do in God's timing. I needed to go through all of my struggles in order to prepare me for walking in my purpose. What I can say is this: Those struggles became a big part of what I do today. Without them, my testimony wouldn't be as powerful as it is.

The seemingly simple decision to start posting inspirational videos was the key that unlocked my purpose for me. Your situation may be different. Understand that finding your purpose is a process. In addition, understand that finding your purpose needs to be a priority. You will not live the life that God has for you until you figure out exactly why you were born into this world. That doesn't happen overnight, trust me. It took me years to find my purpose, but I can truly say that it has been the best thing that has ever happened to me. So I encourage you to be open, and intentional about finding what it is that God has purposed for your life.

Upon finding your purpose, you will begin to see life in a whole different light. It will feel like you have been born again in a sense. That is because you have. Prior to finding your purpose, life is all about you. After you find it, you realize that it is much bigger than just yourself. I believe that God's purpose for each individual involves generations of people. What is the use of giving us gifts and a purpose if all we will do is keep it to ourselves?

Finding my purpose led me to start my first business. It gave me a new confidence that I never had before. If I had not found it, this book would have never come to fruition. Like I said, you are born again when you find out the answer to why you are here. With this new birth comes new ideas, goals, aspirations, and drive. So, have you figured out what it is that you are meant to bring to the world? If not, I encourage you to get in tune with your higher power. Ask for direction and guidance. Ask that your purpose be revealed to you. Your life and the lives of others depend on it.

"I believe I'm here for a reason, and my purpose is greater than any challenges!"
—Unknown Author

Chapter 9 Notes:

_____

_____

_____

_____

_____

_____

_____

_____

_____

_____

_____

_____

_____

Chapter 9 Notes:

The Gift of Restoration

I believe that restoration is one of the most valuable gifts that God gives us. First, let me give you the definition of what it means to be restored. This will help you understand why I am referring to it as a gift. To restore means to bring back, or to reinstate. Another definition is to return someone or something to a former position. Lastly, it can be described as to repair or renovate. A few synonyms for restore are to repair, fix, mend, refurbish, rebuild, or to remodel.

The reason that I say restoration is a gift is that it provides a sense of hope. Knowing that God can restore you, no matter what you've been through, is an awesome feeling. I often hear people say that it is too late for them to find their purpose. Or that they are too old to start doing things differently. This type of thinking is unacceptable. In this book, I have been very transparent about the years I've spent being in my own way. I easily could dwell on that, and choose to remain in the way of my destiny. However, I have realized the power of God and His ability to restore all that I thought I had lost.

Now that you have hopefully learned several ways to get on track and realize your purpose, I want to encourage you to embrace God's restoration process. Rome wasn't built in a day, and neither will the new and improved you. We cannot expect overnight results when it literally took us years to get to where we once were. All of the bad habits, the wrong mindset, the doubt, etc., will take some time to remove from your life. Just know that you are more than able to receive restoration in your life.

"After you have suffered for a little while, the God of all grace [who imparts His blessing and favor], who called you to His own glory in Christ, will Himself complete, confirm, strengthen, and establish you [making you what you ought to be]."
—1 Peter 5:10

Allow me to introduce you to one of my favorite scriptures in the bible. 1 Peter 5:10 (Amplified Bible) says the following: "After you have suffered for a little while, the God of all grace [who imparts His blessing and favor], who called you to His *own* glory in Christ, will Himself complete, confirm, strengthen, and establish you [making you what you ought to be]." The wording in this short verse speaks to my soul. It says a few things to me. One thing is that God's timing is not our timing. When I think of all of the years that I suffered, I say to myself, "I've suffered more than a little while, God." But again, knowing that I am on a different wavelength than God, I began to understand.

The next part of that scripture speaks of God's grace and the fact that He has called us to His own glory in Christ. I talked about purpose in previous chapters, and again I cannot express enough how important it is to find your calling. Finally, the scripture says that God Himself will complete, confirm, strengthen, and establish us. These things will make us who we ought to be. That, to me, is the epitome of being restored. And the fact that God Himself assures us that He will do it makes it even better.

I am currently going through the process of being restored, and I can say firsthand that there's nothing like this experience. There was a time that I felt my life would be nothing but pain and suffering. I wanted to give up so many times. Getting out of my own way seemed impossible. However, now I realize that it was all a part of my process. Everything that we go through is necessary in order for us to become the person that we ought to be. If we skip out on the pain and suffering that we encounter, God will be unable to get the glory that He deserves.

The process of being in your own way, and suffering for a while, makes your story that much greater. Overcoming the obstacle of self opens up a whole new world. It also allows you to look back at how far you have come, and share that testimony with others. Please don't be ashamed to tell someone that you were in your own way for years. That testimony alone may help someone start their process of being restored. There will be some people that will only remember the old you. They'll remember the old you that couldn't seem to get on track. They'll remember the old you that was battered, broken, and seemed to be down for the count. They will not understand the new and improved you. Some will never accept the new you. They will only be able to see you for who you once were, and that is ok.

Consider the Apple iPhone. We all know that Apple is one of the top selling companies when it comes to cell phones, computers, etc. When you see an Apple product, you will at minimum have respect for the product. That is because you know it has a high standard of quality. You may not be a user of their products, but you at least respect the products that they have put out over the years because they have a proven track record.

Now consider the refurbished (or restored) iPhone. This phone was made by the same high-quality company, using the same high-quality parts. It even went through the same process as all of the other brand new phones. The difference in this refurbished phone is that at some point it had some issues. It may have malfunctioned. It may have encountered some water damage. Perhaps the phone had been dropped and was now broken. At that point, it had to be sent back to the creator of the product (Apple) to be worked on and restored to working condition.

Now that the phone is refurbished, it is ready to be sold to someone again. Here is where this analogy gets interesting. When the new owner of this refurbished phone shows it to others, they will have no idea that it is a restored version. They won't see what it has been through simply by looking at it. They will have no clue that it was once broken, battered, and in need of restoration. All they will see is the high-quality Apple product that they know and expect greatness from. The bad things that once happened to this restored product won't be known to others unless the owner shares the story. Compare that to us giving our testimony.

When the owner tells others that their phone is refurbished, there will be mixed reactions. Some will say that the phone isn't as good as a new one. Others will say that it won't last long. You will even have some people say that the refurbished phone can't be used. They will harp on all of the bad things that a restored phone has been through. They will be unable to see the current value in something that has been through so much.

Consider yourself a refurbished product. We have all been through tough times at one point or another. We have endured struggle. We have made sacrifices, and at times been broken. The great thing is that with God, we have the ability to be fully restored to the product that He meant for us to be. Restoration is a process, but it is a process that is well worth going through. After you have been restored, please do yourself a favor: SHARE YOUR STORY!!! Let others know that God has restored you to a position of authority. That even though you were in your own way for years, you have now been put back in position to do great things. Don't worry about the people that will still see the old you. That comes with the territory. Just keep pushing. When others ask what happened to you, let them know that you had a malfunction and had to be sent back to the factory (God) to be refurbished. They may look at you like you are crazy, but you will know exactly what you mean.

In closing, I again thank you for taking the time to read *Step Aside*. It is my sincere prayer that the content in this book has helped you, and will put you on the path to greatness. We have all stumbled in life. There have been times that we all have had doubt, fear, insecurities, etc. The important thing is that we find and maintain a desire to overcome all of those things. Those characteristics will continue to keep us standing in the way of what we are purposed to do. Having said that, take the practical ideas in this book and apply them to your life. I am forever grateful to you for investing in yourself, by investing in me. Until we meet again. God bless you.

Chapter 10 Notes:

_____

_____

_____

_____

_____

_____

_____

_____

_____

_____

_____

_____

_____

_____

Chapter 10 Notes:

Special thanks to my family Curtis McKnight, Roy Jackson Jr., Christopher Williams, Eric Bordley, Craig Bordley, Joy Williams, Eleanor Bordley, Joan McKnight, Cynthia Jackson, Roy Jackson Sr., Kristen and Kim Abney, Kiera Marsh Hall, Kerry Hall Jr., Laila Williams, Paula Williams, Tonetta Dawson, Kesha Hall, Mehki Dawson, Marquise Coleman, Tiera Williams, Handri McKnight, Nadir McKnight, Leatrice McKnight, Tracy Abney, Kevin Abney, Janeen, Janeel, Rodney (Jr. and Sr.), Mark, Kyle, and the rest of my wonderful family. I love you all very much!

I would like to thank Nehemiah Davis, Lauren Tilghman, Ms. Myra Grant, Billionaire PA, Marcus Y. Rosier, Ricky Codio, Jordan Johnson, Billy Abstract, Kimar Cain, George McGowan, Shaun Worthy, Kendall Ficklin, Jahleel Coleman, DaVita Garfield, Sonia Lewis, Leah Dawes, Tamika, Sabrina Washington, Marlene Downing, Ron Green, Chris Arnold, Adil Ismaaeel, Rob Lawton Jr., Stephen Robertson, Troy Davis, and the entire COGA family. You all influenced me to be the best possible version of me.

To my lifelong friends Bryant Brinkley, Douglas Thomas, Roy Butts, Mike Young, Ruffiton Thomas, Irving Jackson, Michael DeShields, Steve, Ronnie, Brad, Mike Josey, Kyle Byrd, Larry Corn, my entire Judson and Bonsall St. family, Carlos Jackson, Kobie Johnson, Baron Jones, Chris Lyons, Vince, Yatt, Vern, Dame, Terrell, Tyrone Reese (R.I.P.), and Tyree Hall (R.I.P.). I thank you all for your love and loyalty throughout the years.

A huge thanks to my Bishop S. Todd Townsend, Pastor Cleo Vilina Townsend, and my Resurrection Center family. To the King's Men of TRC. You all have had such a major impact in my life over the last few years.

Thank You to Steven Taylor Photography for the wonderful cover photo! Your talent never ceases to amaze me!

To everyone else that has played any role in my life I want to thank you as well. Your support means the world to me.

CONTACT KAREEM

Email: INFO@KAREEMLWILLIAMS.COM

Website: WWW.KAREEMLWILLIAMS.COM

 /Kareem L. Williams

 /@kareemlwilliams

 /Kareem Williams